REMOTE FIRST

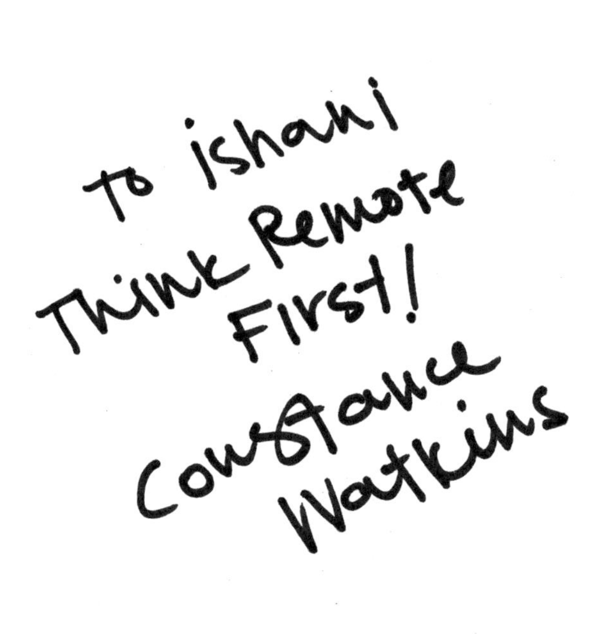

REMOTE FIRST

A MANAGER'S GUIDE TO
BUILDING REMOTE CULTURE

CONSTANCE WATKINS

Remote First Publishing Inc
NEW YORK, NY

First Edition

Book Design by Constance Watkins

The names and identifying characteristics of certain individuals discussed in this book have been changed to protect their privacy.

Published by Remote First Publishing Inc
New York, NY
remotefirstpublishing.com

Printed in The United States of America

ISBN 978-1-7335662-0-9 (casebound)

2 4 6 8 10 9 7 5 3 1

For Jared

Who wanted to read my book long before
I knew I wanted to write it.

CONTENTS

INTRODUCTION

I could have gone into the office. But instead, I was working from my small Midtown Manhattan apartment just six short blocks away. Why? Because the remote culture was more supportive than the traditional office culture.

As the design director for the in-house advertising department of a quick-growing tech startup, I led a team of designers and developers who worked on a high volume of fast-paced projects, often with aggressive timelines. While a few members of my team worked out of traditional offices, the majority were working remotely. My group was spread across seven states, and I had at least one person working in each of the four major U.S time zones. In my leadership position, I was not only tasked with solving the problem of limited time and resources for the day-to-day projects of my team, but also with creating a culture for my people that would keep them motivated and productive, while supporting their individual long-term career development.

In order to create such a culture, I had to work from a remote-first perspective. Though the culture-building solutions of a traditional office could sometimes be adapted to work for a remote team, they weren't designed with remote teams in mind. I needed to come up with remote-specific, culture-building solutions that would work for my group.

By nature, remote work is isolating. So I focused on creating a culture for my team that could be inclusive for all members, regardless of where they worked. I wanted a culture where the members of my team were more collaborative and supported each other. With a supportive remote culture, my team members were better prepared to face the challenges their work presented and handle the stress of the fast-paced environment.

And it worked even better than I'd imagined. As the company grew, my team was able to match the scale of the increased demand; they became more productive and efficient as they worked together. And the remote culture I had created for my team affected me, too. I found that because the remote culture of my team was so supportive,

I was at my most productive when working remotely with them, from my kitchen table with my pet bird on my lap.

I want to help you create a supportive remote culture for your team, too. I know that you're busy with your day-to-day responsibilities, and evolving your team culture takes effort. So, don't waste your effort on trial and error. The practical ideas in this book will equip you to build your best culture.

CHAPTER 1

TAKE CONTROL OF YOUR CULTURE

What is the state of your team's culture right now? Is it productive or dysfunctional? Does your culture encourage communication, or are the members of your team quiet and isolated? Culture is your team's personality. It's shaped by the daily habits of the group members, their communication routines, and how much support they get from each other. If you don't like the state of your team's culture, it's time to take control and shape it into the culture you want it to be.

Your team's culture is powerful; it defines the environment in which your team works. Culture affects the motivation of each of your team members and how engaged they are with their work. When your culture is unsupportive, your team members will be working in isolation, feeling undervalued and unproductive. But a supportive culture will be inclusive, encouraging creativity and collaboration within your team. It will recognize each of your team member's unique value and contributions. A supportive culture will provide an environment in which your team members can be their most productive.

Whether your group is in a traditional office or working remotely, a supportive culture doesn't just happen. Yes, your team will have a culture whether you work to shape it or not. But having a supportive culture takes effort and care.

WHERE DOES CULTURE START?

Team leaders are in a great position to shape their group and positively impact the team's culture. So this book is geared towards leadership. But even if you're not in leadership, keep reading, there is plenty of useful information here for you.

At each stage of your leadership career, you'll be facing different challenges. But no matter where you are, right now is the perfect time to give your team culture some attention.

Maybe you've only been in leadership for a few weeks or months and are now presented with the challenge of developing the culture for your remote team. Or you could be in upper management, working in a traditional office, but wanting to create a healthy environment for the remote teams you lead.

You might still be building your career. Young and ambitious, you know that one day you will take more of a management role. Though you don't directly manage people right now, you are still in a leadership position on your remote team and have enough sway to propose and implement culture-building processes.

Or maybe you are so overloaded with long-term initiatives that the day-to-day leadership that creates a fantastic culture feels too far out of reach for you. No time for trial and error? That's alright, you can implement a few key remote culture-building processes right away.

But wait, what if you're not in leadership at all? Well, here's the thing: I've led teams, worked to shape the culture, and watched the personality of the group evolve. And I'm very aware how much my teams were influenced not just by me, but by each member. Some of the most impactful cultural shifts began with ideas that individuals on my team suggested. So if you're not in a leadership position, don't be discouraged. Keep reading, and see if anything here strikes a chord with you. Take these ideas back and talk about them with your manager. Help build the amazing culture that you and your team deserve.

And leaders: Listen to your people. They are in the trenches and can help you see where your team culture isn't working.

Where does creating a supportive culture begin? Here! Wherever you are right now, whatever position you are in, you will help shape your team's culture.

THINK REMOTE FIRST

I'm going to be walking you through how to create a supportive remote culture, which is something you'll need even if only part of your team works remotely. Because shaping the culture of a remote team is different than shaping the culture of a team in a traditional office, I will focus on some remote-specific culture-building processes. But from time to time, because a strategy that works in a traditional office can be adapted to suit your remote setting, I'll talk about those strategies, too. I'll cover a range of topics, including transparency, communication, friendship, work-life balance, mental well-being, and career development. But I'll start by going over a couple of small shifts that will help you get into a remote first frame of mind.

Culture can be shaped on a company level, but developing the culture that your remote team needs doesn't necessarily have to start on such a grand scale. This book is aimed at your individual team culture, and no matter the size or structure of your company, you'll be able to apply the information contained here. If it is one of the largest in the world, your company may already have culture-building processes in place. If that's the case, the strategies in this book will easily integrate into your existing system. And if your company is small and scrappy, maybe a startup that is just getting off the ground, the processes in this book can guide you as you take the first steps in shaping your remote team's culture.

As you read through the chapters, know that each team is unique. Pay attention to what your people need and how the remote culture-building strategies in this book affect your group. If you work to develop a culture that takes every member of your team into account, you will have a productive environment that your group will enjoy working in.

You are responsible for the quality of your team's culture. Let's get you on your way to making it the one you want it to be!

CHAPTER 2

REMOTE FIRST

Building a supportive culture in a remote environment is very different than building one in a traditional office, so you will need a different approach. In any environment, building a supportive culture begins with communication. But good communication within a remote team doesn't happen by accident; it requires structure and habits that encourage your people to talk.

The most basic of these communication habits is the result of thinking remote first. This means that if anyone on your team is remote from you, you are remote from them, too, even if you're sitting in a traditional office. If anyone is remote, everyone is remote. By simply changing your frame of mind about this one aspect of your team, you'll begin to take steps that will create an inclusive environment for every member of your group, whether they're in the same room as you or across the country.

As you develop remote habits for your team, some may come naturally. Others, though, may feel foreign, and that's alright. It can take time for your team to adjust, but you can do this.

EVERYONE IS REMOTE

Imagine that you're working in a traditional office with a couple of members of your team, but the majority of your group is spread across the country, working remote. On Monday morning, you find yourself catching up with the members of your team sitting in the room with you. You ask about their weekends and tell a funny story about yours. By communicating this way, the bonds between team members are strengthened. But you're not getting to know the team members that aren't in the room. You may be laughing and joking, but the teammates sitting alone in their home offices are isolated from the group.

By thinking remote first as you set up your communication routines, you can prevent a divide from ever happening.

It's important to note that remote first is not quite the same as remote friendly. A remote-friendly environment will accommodate remote work for part of the team either part or all of the time. But the communication routines for a remote-friendly team will closely mirror those of a traditional office. While this may work if your team is only remote from each other for a day or two, now and then, remote-friendly communication won't provide a supportive culture for a team that is working remotely long term. So, let's look more at what you can do to adapt the routines of your team to be remote first.

Structuring your communication is a big part of developing a supportive remote-first culture. In the coming chapters, we'll talk a lot about how you can adjust your communication routines to work for your remote team. For now, start thinking about your team's individual needs. What types of communication would you have in a traditional office? How can you convert those types of communication to work in a remote environment?

A great place to start with remote-first communication is a group chat. In a traditional office, if you want to talk to your team, all you have to do is raise your voice. Your teammates are close enough to hear you. But as a remote worker sitting alone in front of your laptop, you will need a way to communicate with the rest of the group. It's time to find a group chat tool.

If your team already has a group chat in place, that's perfect! But if not, do a bit of research to find one that will fit your group's needs. In its most basic form, a group chat is a text-based place where your group members can all be in the conversation at once. In order to start building your great culture, a basic chat tool may be all you need. But as you're looking through group chat options, you may find there are additional features that would help your team, such as integrated video calling, the ability to archive conversations, or file sharing. As you transition your team to working remote first, you'll be using that group chat a lot, so find one that you will make your day easier.

Working remote first means that everyone acts from a remote mindset, so even if you're sitting in a traditional office with some of the members of your team, conversations should be redirected to the chat. With everything from project updates to group jokes happening in the group chat, verbal conversations in the office will become less frequent. But while the office quiets down, the group chat is going to be lively. With just this one shift in routine, anyone working remote will become more integrated into the group than ever before.

Let's go back to our example of a Monday morning and see what would have happened if the team was working remote first: First thing in the morning, you sit down at your desk next to a couple of your team members working with you in a traditional office. You will probably verbally greet the people in the room, but you also open your group chat to say good morning to your entire team, both the ones in the office with you and the rest of the group working remote.

Everyone starts to add stories about their weekend to the chat; your office is quiet except for the occasional chuckle from the group as you all join the conversation. With this change in your communication routine, your group's conversation isn't divided; everyone on the team is included no matter where they are sitting.

Adjusting your conversation habits to work remote first can take time. If you're feeling awkward, your team probably is, too. But stick with it; you'll find your rhythm! Once you give your remote team a way to communicate, team members will find their voices. They will get to know each other, and the awkwardness will dissipate. They will begin to find ways to support each other, and you will be on your way to building a strong culture for your people.

CAMERA-ON POLICY

A while back, my team was working on a tight deadline for a big pitch. We were all remote and using a group chat to maintain almost constant communication in order to turn out the project as quickly as possible. But from time to time we would run into a problem so complex that trying to explain it in text just caused confusion. When our group chat wasn't enough, it was time to get a few minutes of face-to-face conversation with a video call.

Talking strictly in text can create slow conversations and lead to miscommunications. When a text-based chat becomes confusing, simply hopping on a call can help clear things up, but if your team isn't using video they're not getting the same benefits they would get from in-person interactions.

In a traditional office, if a text-based chat became confusing, you might walk over to the other person's desk for a face-to-face conversation, something you obviously can't do when your team is working remote. But a video call can help you talk through problems, share screens, and gauge each other's reactions, almost as though you were working in the same room with the rest of the group.

So set a camera-on policy for your team. Whether it's a group meeting or just a five-minute check-in between two colleagues, if every call your team members make is a video call you will be giving them one of the benefits of a traditional office they are missing out on by working remotely.

Over time, all of these moments of having the camera on will help your team build an understanding of their teammates and how they communicate. They will become familiar with how everyone turns a phrase or inserts subtle jokes. All of your other communications will benefit from these understandings. If you're so familiar with your team that you can practically hear the other person saying their words as you read them in a chat, you will be able to gather more meaning from a text-based conversation.

A video call can also help you see how the person you're talking to is responding to what you're saying. When you're explaining something complex, do they look confused? Or maybe they understand more that you'd expected and are giving you encouraging nods. Being able to see their response will help you pace yourself appropriately and address confusion if you need to.

With a camera-on policy, your team members may be more empathetic toward each other, be more careful not to talk over each other, and be more polite with their tone. The video connection can be an easy reminder that you're talking to a human and that all of the common in-person etiquette still applies.

The visual connection can also help your remote team stay focused on the call. In a traditional office you'd find a conference room to have conversations, somewhere away from the distractions of the objects on your desk and the people walking by. Working remote can have even more distractions. Not everyone is going to be working from a quiet home office; sometimes remote work happens somewhere noisy, like a coffee shop. Create your focused space—your virtual conference room—with a camera-on policy so that your remote team can get the same benefits as those working in a traditional office, no matter where they're working.

After working remote with a camera-on policy for awhile, you may forget that you've only ever seen your group digitally. You can form friendships, strengthen bonds, and work as a synchronized group, all from your own little corner of the world.

I have a friend I worked closely with for a few years, without ever meeting in person. In that time we chatted continuously through the day and routinely had camera-on meetings. We spent so much time together that we became close, sending holiday gifts and talking about family health. After all those years we had formed a strong friendship without ever being in the same room.

While a camera-on policy is really only for including video any time your team members are on a call, from time to time your group might want the extra level of camaraderie that comes from having an open video call. For example, if you have an intensive day-long project, keeping an open line can help your team continuously support each other. In a traditional office, your group could gather in a conference room and use each other's company to push through the task. But without a conference room for your remote group, an open video call can be a great substitute.

Sometimes your open video call might be quiet, with nothing but the sound of tapping fingers on keyboards. Other times your group may be really active with questions, or jokes and laughter. Some of your group may step away for lunch; others might want to eat at their desks. Sometimes you might see an empty chair or someone picking up their laptop to move to a different room. But whatever the day calls for, your team will be there for each other. This isn't a typical camera-on experience, but not every day is typical. Some days your team might need the extra bonding, for the distance between people to be even shorter.

If you haven't had a camera-on policy with your team before, implementing one can be a big change. You might find a few of your team members are hesitant; after all, part of the appeal of working remote is having the freedom to work in your bathrobe if you want to. Give your group time to adjust before making the change; maybe let them know that you're switching to a camera-on policy the following week.

With any big changes to your team culture, it's important to be consistent. Eventually your team will embrace the changes, and your new routines will become second nature.

CHAPTER 3

TRANSPARENCY

Working remote can feel solitary. Sitting alone in an empty house can leave the members of your remote team disconnected from the big picture and from the rest of the group. But focusing some of your efforts on being transparent can counter their isolation and create a supportive environment. Transparency is about openly relaying the information that your team members need to succeed.

Transparency isn't a concept exclusive to remote work, but being transparent in a remote environment takes extra effort. In a traditional office, the conversations that provide transparency might not need to be quite as overt as in a remote setting; informal project check-ins or course-correcting conversations may happen over a coffee run. But with a remote team where communication is deliberate, being transparent with the information you have will need to be intentional.

Transparency isn't just about being open with your team, but also about gathering the information that you're missing from them. You're the leader, so you'll have more information to share. But knowing the information your team has for you will help you make informed decisions, too. As you're working on your group transparency, ask the questions of your team members that will help you stay informed as well.

Transparency is a broad concept, but you can have the biggest impact on your remote team's culture by focusing your efforts on being transparent with your expectations, your team's unique processes, and the projects that your team is working on.

TRANSPARENT EXPECTATIONS

Expectations come in all sizes. The expectations you have for your team members might be about something as large as the path they need to follow in order to be promoted. But not all expectations are grand. You have expectations about the minutiae of each day, such as participating in group discussions or maintaining a certain level of professionalism with clients. Being transparent with your expectations can give your team members the direction and support they need to be successful with each aspect of their job.

Transparency with expectations starts on everyone's first day of work. When you hire a new team member, you will immediately start sharing what you expect. You will pass along some of your expectations instinctively, like what days or hours you're expecting your team members to work. But other expectations will take a bit more consciousness to make sure you've been clear. Be transparent with your team members about expectations on communication routines. Are you expecting the members of your group to respond to email or pings in the group chat within a certain amount of time? In terms of punctuality, is a 10-minute delay on hitting a deadline acceptable? What about that camera-on policy we talked about in Chapter 2? If you don't tell your team what you're expecting, they might be working with misconceptions.

Focusing some of your efforts on transparency about expectations is important for remote teams because the small, course-correcting, in-person interactions are missing. In a traditional office, the members of your team could observe how others are handling situations, and indirectly gather information about your expectations. For example, in a traditional office, if you had a group meeting and five minutes before it started your entire team stood up to walk to the conference room, any new member of your group would begin to understand the importance of punctuality. But members of a remote team logging onto a video call don't have the same visual cues to prompt them to be punctual. And without you telling them, they may assume that one or two minutes late isn't a big deal.

So how can you be transparent about expectations with your team members? Some expectations, like job descriptions or company policies, will most likely be listed somewhere; make sure your team members have access to that documentation. Other expectations, like how you'd like them to notify you when they are planning to take a long lunch, can be addressed in a quick direct message, or even verbally, maybe in your next one-on-one conversation.

When a member of your remote team is struggling with misunderstood expectations, no one is there to see their misunderstanding and help them. Without transparency in expectations, they might mistakenly assume that they understand what you want and put their efforts in the wrong place. By proactively being transparent with your expectations, you will be giving the members of your team the information and support they need in order to live up to your expectations.

TRANSPARENT PROCESSES

A few years back, my team was fully based in a traditional office where we shared a room with a partner team. The majority of the projects my team worked on followed a strict style guide maintained by members of the partner team, but on occasion a project would need to deviate from the style guide. On these occasions, Elena from my team would turn her chair to Craig from the partner team, who sat directly behind her, to talk through project goals and make sure our teams were aligned on the style guide alterations. With Elena and Craig working in such close proximity to each other, the process for working together was transparent.

Your team's processes will guide the members of your group through each step they take to complete their work. When there is transparency with your team's processes, your team members can make informed decisions. They will have the tools they need to not only make the right choice but to take ownership. Transparency about your team's unique processes will help the individuals in your group know the right person to ask for help in each situation, understand the resources available, and know how their individual work contributes to the big picture. When you are transparent with your people about your team's unique processes, you will be building a culture that supports each member and enables your team to succeed.

Now how would Elena and Craig's situation be different if my team had been fully remote? Without their desks being in proximity, Elena might not have had enough casual conversations with Craig to understand what his role at the company was and how it related to hers. I would have needed to be even more transparent with Elena about what the process was for working with the partner team when she needed to adjust the style guide.

Communication for a remote team is intentional. If your team members don't know the right question to ask, or of whom, they could easily find the wrong answer. In a traditional office, a member of your team could possibly yell "help" across the room and find someone with an answer when they run into a problem. Casual questions can be harder to ask when working remote. The most casual way for a remote team member to ask a question is in a chat. But, somehow, simply writing it down can make the question seem more important than it actually is. This can dissuade members of your remote team from asking simple questions. You can help them avoid this problem by being transparent with your processes.

So, how can you be transparent with your processes? You might want to take process transparency on a case-by-case basis. For instances of unusual projects, like Elena's, walking her through the resources (including Craig) she had available might be the easy solution. But if this type of situation is recurring, you might find that sharing information on a case-by-case basis is cumbersome.

When your processes don't change much from one situation to the next, document them. If you're not sure where to start, ask the members of your team what aspects of your processes are unclear to them. Or notice if you're getting repeat process questions; those areas are a great place to start elaborating.

Once your processes are down on digital paper, share them with your team. Is there a centralized place they will know to look if they need a refresher on what your team processes are? Or will you do a group training? Either way will work, but you can take your process documentation a step further and get your group involved.

By having members of your team take ownership of maintaining and updating individual aspects of the process documents, you will be enabling each of them to become a team expert in their area. They will be able to let the group know when a process has changed or been updated and will have become so knowledgeable on their individual process area that they'll be able to answer questions if other members of the group are unclear. Giving ownership of the documentation to your team will not only help you be transparent with the members of your team, it will also make them devoted to helping you maintain the transparency around your team's processes.

By being transparent with your team's unique processes, you will be giving each member of your team the information they need to make informed decisions as they go through their work day. And by getting them involved in perpetuating the transparency, you will not only have a very informed team but a supported one as well.

TRANSPARENT PROJECTS

Late one Friday afternoon, one of the Account Managers from the sales team reached out to me with a project that he had forgotten to submit for design. There were six line items and it was due back to the client before the end of the day. The turnaround was tight, but I figured if I had two designers each take half of the project we could still make the deadline. I talked to Ben and Tara; they split up the line items and set to work. But there was a miscommunication: Both Ben and Tara thought that they were responsible for the top half of the list. Unknowingly, they were duplicating work.

This type of miscommunication could happen in any work environment. But if you had two team members working near each other in a traditional office, they could discover the miscommunication more quickly than if they were working remotely. One might glance at the other's screen and notice that they were both working on the same line item, or one might ask a quick directional question about how the other was handling an element in his portion, and the small talk could bring the misunderstanding to light. But working remotely on a tight deadline, they both would most likely take their portion and work in isolation until they were done.

Transparency in projects gives each person involved the information they need in order to make the project a success. You can do this by detailing the portion of the project each team member is responsible for, who else is involved, and when the other team members' portions of the project come in to play. Help your team understand the scope of the project and the resources available. Give them what they need to make informed choices as the project progresses, and ultimately, to work together to make the project a success.

A lack of transparency about projects can make anyone feel like they are working in the dark, which can be frustrating, even disheartening. The more transparency you can provide to your team about the projects they are responsible for, the more smoothly and successfully the projects will progress.

How can you introduce transparency into projects? On a very small scale, the answer could be as easy as keeping the lines of communication open, discussing the project frequently throughout the duration, and keeping everyone involved in the project up to speed on the project's progress. But if you're dealing with projects on a larger scale, which you most likely are, implementing a workflow system is a great solution.

AGILE WORKFLOW SYSTEM

The agile workflow system emphasizes daily check-ins, rapid iteration, ease of altering scope, and overall project transparency. This system is popular in software development because it focuses on small accomplishments, allowing projects to pivot quickly if the end goal changes. But whether or not you're in software development, the agile workflow system works especially well for a remote team because it includes communication processes that will help bridge the distance between the members of your remote group.

Two elements of the agile workflow system will help you keep transparency in your team's projects: a project board and a standing daily meeting called *scrum*. The agile workflow system is more complex than this, and if you're interested there are a lot of resources out there. But in terms of transparency in projects, these two elements are the most useful.

The project board is a place where everyone on the team can see, at a glance, the scope and progress of a project. This makes it easy for someone new to the project to step in and be able to lend a hand within a few minutes. This level of transparency will help your team take ownership of a project and show individual team members how their work fits into the whole. Depending on how you set up your project board, you can also include information about anyone who worked on previous steps of the project and anyone scheduled to work on the subsequent steps.

In its simplest form, the project board is broken out into three columns: "To Do," "Doing," and "Done." All of the team's projects are sorted into the appropriate column and each individual project moves from one column to the next as it is completed. In a traditional office, this could be represented with sticky notes on a wall. But for your remote team, you'll probably want to use a project management tool, such as Trello or Asana.

The other element of the agile workflow system that will help you maintain transparency with your team is scrum. Sometimes also called a daily standup, scrum is a daily standing meeting where everyone on your team gets together to talk about their projects. In turn, each member of your team should discuss what they worked on yesterday, what they are planning on working on today, and anything that is standing in the way of their progress.

The term *scrum* is borrowed from rugby and was first used in a January 1986 *Harvard Business Review* article by Hirotaka Takeuchi and Ikujiro Nonaka, "The New New Product Development Game," to reference the importance of how team members interplay in order to allow for speed and flexibility of product development. Within the agile workflow system, scrum emphasizes the importance of working together as a group. This short, standing meeting does just that; scrum can open up the channels of communication for your remote team and encourage your people to work together. These daily check-ins keep the whole team on the same page, and can give your group the opportunity for quick discussions on how to clear any roadblocks your team members are up against.

As you incorporate a project board and scrum into your routine, you may notice that the projects discussed in your daily meeting are exactly the same as the ones on your project board. This is perfect! The purpose of using a project board and scrum together is to maintain transparency with your group's projects. While transparency can feel like over communication at times, with a remote team over-communication is often exactly what you need to make sure everyone in your group is informed.

CHAPTER 4

COMMUNICATION

Have you ever been on an email thread with someone you're not completely familiar with? Maybe a client, a freelancer, or even the family doctor? The flow of the conversation is formal, each of you only saying what you absolutely need to say. But how would the conversation change if you were able to become more familiar with each other? What extra information would you volunteer or receive if the tone became slightly less formal?

Does that short, concise email thread reflect the type of conversation the members of your team have? If so, they're missing out on opportunities to support and learn from each other. Without structures that encourage casual interactions, the members of your team may never really get to know each other. They may never form good working relationships or communication habits.

The way your team communicates is a huge indicator of how healthy your team culture is. Are team members open with each other about what they need in order to complete their work? Or are they so intimidated by each other that they can't collaborate? How much support is each individual getting from you and the rest of your team? A healthy team culture will support its members. Good communication is the cornerstone.

Without good communication, the members of your team may become disengaged because of a lack of support. If team members don't have the opportunity to get to know each other, they may never be comfortable enough to be candid. They'll give and get only the specific information asked for. They won't ask small directional questions, and collaboration won't happen.

This lack of communication can extend to your interaction with the members of your team as well. If the conversations you have with team members are only during scheduled meetings, small successes may go unrecognized, and behavioral problems can incrementally escalate. Team members may perceive you, their leader, as apathetic towards their efforts. How can you lead them if they don't look to you for support?

But don't worry! You can encourage routines that will build familiarity between the members of your remote team and help your culture be supportive. Formal meetings, emails, and project updates will always be a valuable part of a productive team. But you also need to create some extra time for your people to talk and get to know each other. In a traditional office, it's easy to bump into a teammate in the hall and make small talk, which is where the familiarity between teammates begins. What can you do to help build that same sort of familiarity with your remote team? How can you help your group to loosen up?

COMMUNICATING IN REAL TIME

When you work remote, you're invisible. You can easily fall into communication routines that reinforce your invisibility: only responding to email in the last hour of the day, seeing a direct message come in and not responding right away, or even noticing that an important conversation is happening in the group chat and not joining in, but adding your thoughts hours after the fact. Delayed communication habits like this increase invisibility and can make your culture feel cold.

If everyone on your team delays their communication, everyone will be working unsupported. When they ask a question in the group chat, they may have no benchmark for how long it will take for a response. It can seem like asking a question to an empty room and crossing your fingers for an answer. This isn't going to lead to a collaborative environment.

Have you ever played video games online as a team, maybe Halo or Overwatch? Teams that play video games aren't all that different from remote teams. No one is in the same room or looking at the same screen, but all have a common goal. The team members are all working together to succeed. Members of video game teams put on headsets and stay in constant communication; without that they couldn't win. If one of them came across radio silence, they would almost immediately fall out of sync with the rest of the group. If one member stepped away to make dinner without telling the rest of the team, what would it be like when the next battle started and he was missing? How would the group react? Would they think he'd been disconnected? Is he mad? Is he going to be there to have their back?

Of course, remote teams don't need the same level of intensity with their real-time communication as the teams that play video games. You don't need a headset and an open channel all day every day. But knowing that your team has your back when you need them is a big part of a supportive culture. For example, if your team doesn't know that they'll be able to get an answer to their question in time to act on it, will they ask the question at all? Or will they simply turn to Google and hope for the best?

Allowing the people on your team to feel isolated because of ineffective team communication habits will work against you as you try to build a supportive team culture. So how can you get your group to communicate in real time rather than on a delay?

The answer starts with you. You lead the group, and its members look to you to set the standard. In a traditional office, they could glance at your desk and see that it's empty. But for a remote team, that isn't an option. So, drop a note in your group chat to let your team know when you're stepping away for coffee or headed into hours of back-to-back meetings. If you're going to log out of the group chat for awhile in order to give your undivided attention to a project, tell the team before you do. Giving your team a bit of insight into when you'll be unavailable will help them understand that you're not ignoring them when they raise a question.

On a larger scale, a shared calendar can also give the group insight into the availability of each team member. If everyone on the team understands when teammates are scheduled to be away, they can plan their communication accordingly.

Let's say, for example, that you have a designer and developer who have been working on a project together for the last few weeks. One Monday morning, the developer runs into a problem and sends a message to the designer about it. And then he waits. And waits... and waits. The designer isn't responding. Did she understand what the developer was asking? Should he elaborate on his question? It is early on a Monday; is she just late for work? Should he continue to wait? By lunch, your developer still hasn't received a response. What should he do?

With a shared calendar, your developer could take a look at the designer's schedule and see if she is on vacation for the day or simply in meetings that are delaying her response. With the extra information about her schedule, he can work accordingly. If she's scheduled to be back online in the afternoon, maybe he can wait for an answer to his question. But if she's set to be on vacation for the next few days, he may need to look elsewhere for the answers he needs.

I should point out that in this scenario, the designer could have been a bit more transparent with her schedule beforehand. If she's working closely with a developer and knows that she's going to be away, sending him a note before she logs off would have been ideal. But oversights happen, and a shared calendar for the group can provide an added layer of real-time information.

As your group gets into the habit of communicating in real time, they will develop a level of visibility, which will help them get to know each other and feel supported. And that is a big part of what developing your culture is about.

THE FIVE-MINUTE VIDEO CALL

For a remote team, the easiest forum for quick communication is a text-based chat, whether as a group or in a direct message. But what if a text-based chat isn't enough? What do you do when the question becomes complex enough that it's tough to find the right words, and miscommunications begin to happen? In a traditional office, you can lean to your neighbor and talk it through. But how can you have a face-to-face conversation when your team is remote?

Hop on a video call, of course! It doesn't have to be formally scheduled or last for a significant amount of time. If a question comes up and it's just too complex to work through in a text-based chat, make a call. Take advantage of the camera-on policy we talked about in Chapter 2. See the face of the person you're talking to, and let them see yours. Hear their tone. So much understanding can come from really talking to someone.

If your team members aren't familiar with each other, you may notice some pushback on incorporating these quick face-to-face conversations into their routines. When you know the person you're talking to, it's less intimidating to ask questions, especially questions that may seem silly or insignificant. If you're friends with the person on the other end of the call and understand what they're going through on their project, you can also give unsolicited but relevant information without it being perceived as intrusive. So how can you get your group comfortable enough to hop on a call?

Short meetings that include your entire team can give just a bit of space for your people to get to know each other. A lot of conversation can happen in the few minutes before a meeting officially starts. Those few minutes of shuffling about as the team waits for everyone to join the call is a great space for familiarity to form. It isn't much time, but sometimes it's all you need to begin to loosen up. Scrum, which we talked about in Chapter 3, is a great place for this to start.

If your team isn't already in the habit of video calls, or are unfamiliar with the software they have access to, they may feel a bit of hesitation. It can be frustrating to have a question that you know will only take a few minutes to talk through, ask someone to hop onto a call, and discover they don't have the software installed. All of a sudden your five-minute call has taken 30 minutes. So take the time to help your team members with a little setup and training about the software and encourage them to incorporate quick video calls into their routine.

The conversations that your team will have once they get into the habit of a five-minute video call will help them really get to know and trust each other. They will be able to avoid confusion and miscommunication from text-based conversations and be able to collaborate together more effectively.

FEEDBACK

With a remote team, the importance of giving little pieces of feedback can easily be overlooked. When your communication habits with your team are limited to formal meetings or email threads, opportunities to give incremental feedback can be overlooked.

Feedback is part of a supportive team culture. So missing the opportunities to give incremental feedback, whether good or bad, will affect your entire group dynamic. Feedback shapes both individual growth and group success, supporting overall job satisfaction.

In a traditional office, if a team member did a good job, he or she would get a bit of attention. If it was something small, like spending five minutes fixing that bug in the code that no one had gotten around to yet, the team member might get a high-five. Positive feedback isn't necessarily always grand; not every job well done will earn a plaque or trophy. But giving a bit of recognition will let your team member know that his work didn't go unnoticed.

Chances are, once you start looking, you'll find a lot of opportunities where you can give a bit of positive feedback. This is great! But wait ... you're remote and can't give a high five. So, what will you do? Are there remote-specific feedback channels you can take advantage of? If the positive feedback is for something small, maybe you could send a GIF of a high five. Or maybe you'd like to call more attention to your team member's success, in which case, is there an appropriate group email that you could include kudos in? If the feedback is for something really great, this could be a perfect time to take advantage of that five-minute call to express a sincere "thank you."

Of course, not all feedback is good. For remote leadership, it can be tempting to hold off on negative feedback until a standing one-on-one meeting. But a delay in giving small, incremental feedback can deepen the issue. If small issues are neglected long enough, they can easily grow into bigger problems.

I had a new team member who, after a few months on my team, started missing deadlines by 10 minutes. The first few times, I thought the delay was an oversight on his part. But after a week, he was constantly late with his work. When I didn't let him know my expectations right away, he thought that his timelines were totally acceptable and began pushing the boundary even further. By waiting to address the issue, I was unintentionally reinforcing his bad behavior. After that first week, I realized my mistake: The situation wasn't going to resolve itself. I needed to be direct with my feedback.

Confusing feedback is almost as bad as no feedback at all. The most common muddled message that you can send is in the form of a feedback sandwich, also known as a crap sandwich. This technique is when one piece of negative feedback is "sandwiched" between two pieces of positive feedback. For example: "The design that you did for the

Waterman project was great, but it was turned in so late that we couldn't use it. But your design was really creative." This type of feedback is confusing. Does the recipient act on the positive or the negative? Was the job acceptable or not?

Sandwiching feedback is confusing for employees in a traditional office but even more so for remote employees. Reading between the lines of a conversation can be especially challenging if feedback conversations are infrequent. So be direct. If you have positive feedback, give that. And if there's negative feedback, be direct about that, too. Don't try to gloss over the problem or soften the blow.

If you address feedback as soon as you see the need for it, your team will know where you stand. Delaying positive feedback can make your team members feel undervalued. And putting off giving negative feedback can reinforce bad habits. But if you're direct and honest with the members of your team about their performance, they will be able to learn and grow.

The way your group communicates will affect your overall team culture. Incorporating habits that increase visibility, encourage face-to-face communication, and address feedback needs when they arise will help you develop a culture that supports the members of your team.

CHAPTER 5

FRIENDSHIP

In the last chapter we talked about how difficult communication can be for remote teams. In a traditional office, the conversations that are the base for forming friendships happen simply because people are in the same space. But for a remote team, all of the communication is intentional. Without structures and routines that encourage communication, remote workers will never accidentally run into someone and strike up a conversation the way that traditional office workers might. And because of this, remote team members may never loosen up and actually get to know the people they are working with. A job isn't just about the work; people want to feel like they're part of a team.

A while back, I had a team member who was falling behind. He had some bad habits that were creating long hours of extra work for the rest of the group. If he hadn't cared about his teammates, he might not have had any problem putting this extra pressure on them. But the friendships within my group were strong, and solving this problem was as simple as talking to him about the stressful situation he was creating for his teammates. He was so dedicated to them that finding out he was putting them in a tough spot changed his actions almost immediately. Because I helped to create a strong sense of community within my group, my team had a culture where the members supported and looked out for each other.

CASUAL CONVERSATIONS

In a traditional office, friendships grow out of casual conversations that begin simply from sharing space with each other. For a remote group, developing routines that encourage communication may be the only way that those friendship-forming conversations happen. If the group chat has been silent for days or weeks, members of your team may hesitate before they add a comment, and the silence will continue. So, what can you do to break the ice?

Give your team space to laugh and joke together. Create routines that will get them talking so they feel comfortable with each other. Even a small comment in a group chat can cut the tension. If you lead the way with a joke, the rest of the group will laugh. And then they'll follow your lead. My last team could always get a great conversation going by sharing a bad ad. But a GIF of a kid rubbing ice cream on his face works just as well.

A quick game of Free Association Emoji first thing in the morning can be a great way to get daily conversations started. In Free Association Emoji, someone adds an emoji to the group chat, and then everyone sticks with the theme and adds her or his own. The way that each member of the team interprets what they think the theme is can throw silly twists into the game.

So, how can you get a game of Free Association Emoji started for the first time? The most blunt way is to be direct with your group and tell them how to play before you kick the game off. Or you could keep it subtle and let the game evolve on its own. First thing in the morning add an emoji. Maybe a simple wave or something that reflects the weather where you are. Even without telling the rest of the team how the game is played, they should pick it up within the first week. But if they don't, enlist someone to play along. Once it becomes routine for the team, unspoken rules will form: Who goes first? Are do-overs allowed? Is there a time limit?

The rules will be unique to your team. The structure will evolve to suit them. And this is perfect!

In the last group I led, adding the first emoji was always a race; being the one to get the theme going was coveted. The unspoken rule was that the first emoji couldn't be added until after 10 a.m. Eastern. The second the clock turned, the game would start. If you let the members take ownership, the rules will become unique to your team, and everyone will want to be involved.

Don't let your group chat be silent for an entire day, if it is, your team members are most likely working in isolation. A silly GIF may be enough to break the ice when you need it, but a routine that the members of your group can own would be even better. If they're having fun, you won't have to shoulder all of the responsibility for casual conversations and building camaraderie within your group. If you create routines that the group likes, they will perpetuate them. These routines don't need to be grand; they can be as small as getting a daily conversation going in your group chat.

STORYTIME

Traditional offices always have a place where people can congregate. It may be the coffee machine, the sparkling water fountain, or the office cafe. This place is communal. It offers a space for teammates to talk about what is happening in their lives, to learn about each other, find shared interests, and connect.

Remote workers can't just stand up and walk to their kitchen for a glass of water and find the same sense of community. So, how can you create this space for your team? How can you bring your people together to share a story with each other, to bond?

A meeting called Storytime can be your digital water cooler. Storytime is a daily standing video call where your team can come together and talk about what's going on. A lot of bonding can happen between your team members in 20 minutes a day.

Storytime is informal; it can have as much or as little structure as you need to get your team talking. You can set it up as a meeting with a guided discussion or just allow the conversation to flow naturally. The topics don't have to be full of personal details, but if someone wants to talk about the problems they're having with their neighbors, more than likely the rest of the group will be able to relate.

In its simplest form, one person can tell a story, and the conversation evolves from there. Each member of your team can contribute by adding a story of their own. One Storytime that stands out to me from a previous team of mine started with me sharing a story of my weekend and how I had a stunt-worthy mishap with my new motorcycle that led to a Sunday in the emergency room and nine stitches to fix the gash on my chin.

From there, the chat about weekend events continued with another teammate sharing how she had learned to throw axes that Saturday. Within a few minutes, the conversation had evolved into a discussion of such extreme hobbies that we were debating who would be the last survivor of the zombie apocalypse. This particular conversation happened after my group had been participating in Storytime for the better part of a year, so don't worry if you can't get your people to open up that much right away. The first few times your team gets together for Storytime, the conversation may feel awkward, but as you continue you'll get to know each other and your dynamic will improve.

So, you're on a call. Cameras on. Staring at each other. In silence. Who is going to get things going? You might want to start on a volunteer basis; if someone has something to share let her speak up. Though with this method, some days the silence may go on for a while. If one of your team members just got back from vacation or did something exciting over the weekend that you know about, you could invite him to share a story. Or you could have designations: on Mondays, Carmen tells the first story, on Tuesdays it's Mark's turn, and so on. You could even turn it into a game: Whoever logged onto the call first gets to choose someone to tell the first story.

If your team is still stumped for conversation, an easy way you can get things moving is to pose a question that everyone can relate to but will have a unique answer to. Maybe a question about weekend plans; you all have a weekend, what will you do? Or first jobs. You are professionals now, but what did you do for money when you were young? Was it a paper route? Or working retail at a local tuxedo shop? What happens when you find that two members of your team, living on opposite coasts of the country, worked the same first job? That's a bond forming! If you run out of questions before the conversations have started to evolve on their own, search for a list of conversation starters.

For strong bonds to form within your group, your people will need time to come together. Your group has similarities; after all, you've found yourselves all working on the same team at the same company. You're all working remote; if nothing else, that is something you have in common. Storytime is a place to find out more about who you're working with and to help each individual in your group develop a sense of belonging to the team.

HAPPY HOUR

Once your team members have developed friendships, they may want to spend even more time together. In a traditional office, people start off as work friends, sharing a joke in the break room or going to lunch. But eventually the friendships become strong enough that they spend time together outside of work—maybe stopping at the bar before heading home, starting a group bowling league, or meeting up to watch the game on Saturday afternoon. But for a remote team, sitting around and hanging out without some sort of structure can be difficult.

Adding an informal hour, or Happy Hour, at the end of the week can be just the space you need. It can be the loosest meeting that anyone has on their calendar. Not mandatory by any means. And not exclusive. If friends or family are around, invite them, too. Everyone is welcome.

Despite the casual format, put it on the calendar. Make it easy for your team members to find and attend. If it fits with their schedule, awesome! And if not, no worries. It's just one extra venue that they can take advantage of to build friendships and strengthen team bonds.

So, now you have some time set aside, what will you do? Depending on your company policies, it might be as simple as everyone cracking open a beer. But there are plenty of things you can do that don't involve alcohol. The world is getting smaller, and there are so many ways for people to come together remotely. Will you log into a video call and play trivia? Maybe you want to start a Fortnite league (the digital version of a bowling league) or take the time to share your hobbies—like one person teaching the group to make homemade pasta or one teammate giving everyone a tarot reading. Everyone has something they're interested in. Where will these interests intersect for your team?

If you're stumped, check out Jackbox.tv. They have a great selection of group games, including Quiplash and

Drawful. With everyone logged onto a video call, one person can host the game and share the "board" by sharing their screen. From there, everyone will need their phone handy to play their turn. Jackbox.tv games always start with a tutorial, so you'll be able to quickly get everyone up to speed, and you'll be set to go.

If your activity can bring people face to face, that is awesome! If you're doing an online gaming group, face to face may not be an option, and that works too. You know your team. You do you. But once they become friends, your team will want to get together. And if you give them a venue, they'll pick it up and run with it.

As you integrate community-building routines into your day, if one of them doesn't work, don't stress. Your team is unique, so not all activities will suit your group. There is always another one that will. Be open with your group: Ask them what they like. If they don't like these, is there something they'd rather do? Their answer may be something that you couldn't have anticipated, such as a time-restricted design challenge once a week using whatever tools you have available, be it pencil, photoshop, or css animation. And by your involving them in the choice, they will be able to take a bit of ownership, becoming more invested in team bonding than they otherwise would have.

Remember the team member I mentioned at the beginning of the chapter who was falling behind? Because he felt supported by the group, once he was aware of the problem he had been creating for his teammates, he was comfortable enough to ask for help when he needed it. He felt a sense of responsibility toward the team. By creating a sense of community within my group, the problem didn't escalate. If you can get your people talking, your remote workers will no longer be isolated; they may be a world apart, but they will be working with their friends.

CHAPTER 6

WORK-LIFE BALANCE

Up to this point, we've been talking about building a culture that brings your people together so they can collaborate and be their most productive. With your team members supporting each other, you will have a culture where they're happy and want to work. This is awesome! They will enjoy what they do and who they're working with. So much so, in fact, that you may have a tough time getting them to step away at the end of the day. I've had team members who wouldn't log off for the weekend or schedule vacations. While I appreciated the extra hours they were putting in, I knew that if they continued with the late days they were bound to burn out.

Work-life balance is about finding the equilibrium between working toward success and supporting your own self-care and happiness. So, work-life balance is really just about how much time in the day is spent on work and how much is left to spend on personal activities such as family, entertainment, and relaxation.

Achieving work-life balance involves finding the times when you need to stay on task and finding the times when you need to get up and walk around or change focus. It can feel weird to step away from work for lunch, especially if you're not really going to move from your kitchen table where you've been working. But allowing for the distinction between the time when you're hard at work and the moments when you can step away will allow you to come back with a fresh view of the task at hand. This can be a benefit for everyone on your team.

Remote workers notoriously overwork themselves. When you've been working from your couch for the last 10 hours, you may have trouble leaving work behind to "go home" at the end of the day. This can be even harder if you love what you do and are enjoying yourself. But even if your team is happy with the long hours in the moment, helping them find a good work-life balance can prevent stress and burnout in the long run. So, what can you do? How can you help them find their balance?

LEAD BY EXAMPLE

When working remote, setting personal work boundaries is trickier than it would be in a traditional office. For traditional office workers, the change in space of leaving the office at the end of the day can create a clear boundary.

You can help define the boundaries for your remote team by maintaining a good work-life balance yourself. Your team is looking to you to lead the way. Do you already have habits that support a good work-life balance? If so, how can you be open with your team about some of those habits?

You might find that calling out when you're stepping away for coffee or lunch will help remind others that they've been sitting for too long and need to stretch their legs. If you're the one that's not stepping away for coffee or lunch, you might want to find time to stretch your legs, too. These moments away from your laptop will help you come back to projects with a fresh view, help you reduce stress, and support your personal work-life balance.

Boundaries for calling it a day aren't as clearly defined for remote workers as they are in a traditional office. Don't just blend the work day with the evening; step away when you're done. Drop a note in the group chat to let your team know that you're logging off for the evening, or that unless it's urgent you'll respond to outstanding email or chat messages in the morning. Even if there is one last project that you need to finish up before morning, or your inbox really is just too full to call it a day, you can always log back in later. But show (don't just tell) your team that it's okay to disconnect, to go and eat dinner, to spend time with family, to be done for the night. This is a great way to define the boundaries that will support work-life balance for your remote team.

You may find you have a few employees who consistently overwork. This is a common problem with remote workers, a problem I have dealt with frequently. One example is Dylan, a member of my team who was routinely working long hours. He was the first one online in the morning and, even though he had finished with his workload long before the end of the day, he would get a jumpstart on future projects and stay online for hours after everyone else had logged off. I began to worry that these long hours would lead to stress or cause the quality of his work to deteriorate. Or that he might even face burnout.

I had a conversation with him about work-life balance and encouraged him to step away at the end of the day. But he explained that his wife worked long hours away from home, and without the distraction of work, he was lonely. He assured me that he'd let me know if he began to feel overworked, but right then, these long hours created balance for him. I had done what I could. Dylan was aware that I was concerned about his work-life balance, and I understood the position he was in. As time went on, we continued to discuss work-life balance, and ensured that he remained in a healthy balance.

If someone on your team is routinely caught up with their projects, or already ahead of schedule and is simply spinning their wheels at the end of each day, a gentle reminder may help them remember to disconnect. Don't force it though. Everyone deals with work-life balance differently, and leading by example to help them understand that you support finding their balance is sometimes the best thing you can do. From there, it is up to them to create their own boundaries.

DIVERSIONS

People working in a traditional office often find time for diversions: a few minutes of ping pong with a coworker, running to the local coffee shop with a teammate, or small conversations throughout the day on topics like sports, the silly thing their cat did last night, or recanting last night's episode of *American Idol* and all of the injustices in it. Moments like this can offer just enough distraction to help them come back to work even more focused than before. These moments happen because people have formed friendships with their colleagues.

Work friendships, and the diversions during the workday that they bring, can help support the "work" part of work-life balance. When your team members have good working relationships with each other, they will be more likely to support each other. And having time to chat with colleagues about topics not related to work can help relieve stress. Sometimes turning focus away from a tricky problem for a couple of minutes to talk about the difference between yams and sweet potatoes can give your team enough of a break to see the problem differently when they turn their focus back to work.

It can be hard for close work friendships to organically form in a remote team. When you're always separated by a laptop, the communication between teammates may feel overly formal or distant. If they don't know that everyone else on the team owns a cat, they might not talk about that really strange cat toy that they just bought. They might not find out that they share a unique hobby such as bread making or astrology with someone else on the team. If they don't know that others on the team like college basketball, they might not think to form a March Madness group with their remote coworkers. Small similarities like these are the foundation for making work friends. So, what can you do to encourage friendships to form? How can you help break the ice?

Storytime and Happy Hour, both discussed in Chapter 5, are great tools to help encourage a bit of fun within your group. Setting both of these as standing meetings can help your remote team get to know each other. But sometimes you can't wait for your 2 o'clock meeting to share a GIF of otters holding hands, and let's be honest, everyone could use a moment of fun with those otters to brighten their day.

Moments of fun between teammates can directly affect work-life balance. When days are filled with nothing but focused work for hours upon hours, week after week, burnout is inevitable. A few minutes of off-topic conversations with teammates throughout the day can give your team members time to rest, allowing them to recharge enough to be able to carry on with more focused work. While scheduled group activities, such as Storytime, can give your team guaranteed time to come together each day, the need to momentarily divert attention in order to maintain work-life balance doesn't run on a schedule.

Creating a digital space such as a group chat for off-topic conversations can provide a venue for quick diversions and moments of fun throughout the day. Maybe it's a space for everyone to talk about their pets or share their favorite taco recipe. When one person needs a quick change of pace from the task at hand, she can turn to the group chat. The whole team could find a moment of relaxation from that one person's need for a break. Those LOL's aren't going to happen on their own, but encouraging fun within your group will help get you there. You know your team; what do you think would help bring them together? What do they have in common? How can you encourage small diversions and facilitate moments of fun?

Take it upon yourself to get the conversation going. This can be as simple as carrying the topic from today's Storytime into the group chat so that the team can continue to talk even though the call has ended. Or, if you know that your group has an affinity for llamas, daily taking a moment to share a llama fact could get your group engaged in a conversation.

At one point I had a team that enjoyed debating the best way to make coffee, so every morning I'd get the conversation going by talking about how I'd prepared my morning cup. If your group chat is generally silent, your team members might feel they need to keep the topics formal. But with you leading the way, the group chat can become a space for your team to have a bit of fun. If you get the ball rolling, your team members will join in and may even eventually take the initiative to get the conversation going themselves.

You might find that your team easily has fun together. If so, this is perfect! But you may find that you have a quiet bunch. Offering a bit of structure in the beginning can help this space get up and running. The structure could be as simple as starting your morning by adding a coffee GIF or a picture of a sunrise. As your group chat is getting off the ground, your participation will help this digital space grow. Having fun fits any culture, but a remote culture often needs a bit of help to make sure it happens.

STAGGERED WORK HOURS

It's time for you to start your day. You log into your group chat and catch up on all of the conversations you missed. It's first thing in the morning, but because your team is working staggered hours, a great deal of work has been done since you logged off last night.

If your team was in a traditional office, team members would probably show up for the day within 5 or 10 minutes of each other and walk out the door at the end of the day as a group. But for a remote team working across a number of time zones, it's common to work staggered hours, with some team members stepping away for lunch at the same time others are just starting their day.

Staggered hours can can solve a lot of problems, such as being able to hire the perfect person for the job despite his time zone, or accommodating individualized work schedules for your team members, allowing them to find their individual work-life balance. But a lot of the communication that creates a supportive culture is more challenging with staggered hours than it would be if your team was always online at the same time.

If your group is working staggered hours, group members won't have as much overlapping time for communication. And without communication they will start to feel like they're working in isolation. They won't be supporting each other, and they won't be able to develop camaraderie and friendships as easily as if they were all online at the same time.

I had a team that, although fully remote, was based in one time zone. With the whole team working the same schedule, it was easy to set our daily group meetings at a time that worked for everyone. But as the team grew, I hired new team members in a variety of time zones and adopted staggered hours. In order for the entire team to come together for our standing team meetings, such as scrum and Storytime (see Chapters 3 and 5, respectively), the meetings had to be rescheduled during our overlapping time.

Because the window of overlap was so narrow, finding a timeslot that worked for the entire team was challenging. So I recommended removing the team meetings from the calendar and instead using our group chat for a quick daily check-in. Wow! That was an unpopular idea. Almost everyone on my team came to me individually to express how much they relied on the face time they got with the rest of the team during our daily team meetings. So, working with the members of my team, I rearranged schedules and found a time that would work for the entire group.

Take advantage of the time you have together. Focus on the communication and team-bonding routines that are most effective for your group. Since a daily scrum and Storytime were the meetings that brought my team together best, I made sure to schedule them at a time when the entire group could attend. But if coming face to face for those two meetings isn't the most beneficial for your team, find another way to use your overlapping time to bring your people together. Culture, of course, isn't the only priority you'll need to focus on during your overlapping time. But with your limited time together, do something each day that will support the overall cultural health of your team.

While staggered hours can help support individual work-life balance by helping your team members work a schedule appropriate to their time zone, without boundaries, staggered hours can also make work-life balance hard to maintain. For example, Sophia works on the East Coast and has already put in a full day at work. But Mike works on the West Coast, and he's going to be online for a few more hours after Sophia calls it a day. As he runs into questions with the project they're working on together, he starts to drop notes into a direct message with her.

This situation can easily interfere with Sophia's work-life balance in one of two ways. First, it's possible that she's trying to spend her evening resting and relaxing so she can return to the project in the morning with a fresh perspective, and those direct messages are pulling her back to work. Solving this work-life balance challenge can be as easy as setting boundaries on individual after-hours messaging or encouraging your team to take advantage of the built in "set as away" feature that most chat tools have.

The second way this situation could interfere with Sophia's work-life balance is if she is so excited about the project that, while technically done for the day, she is still lurking. She's keeping an eye on the progress that Mike is making and is messaging him back. While this might help the project move along more quickly, it isn't a sustainable approach to Sophia's work-life balance. At this point, it would be good to give Sophia a gentle reminder to disconnect at the end of the day. And beyond that, keep an eye out for signs of burnout and be prepared to address that if it arises. (See Chapter 7 for more on Burnout.) The best way to avoid staggered hours leading to overwork and burnout among your people is to be proactive about your policy. After your policy is in place, be aware of when you have people working long hours so you can help them find their work-life balance. If you're not sure that long hours are happening, look for signs such as projects moving more quickly than expected, after-hours conversations in the group chat, or signs of the beginning of burnout, such as increased interpersonal problems, frustration, issues with job performance, or a change in motivation or enthusiasm. But really, one of the easiest ways to know about after-hours work happening is if you have open channels of communication with your people. Talk to them. They'll most likely come out and tell you that they've been doing extra work.

Staggered hours can present a challenge with communication routines. But if you focus your efforts on how your team communicates when they are all online together, they will still be able to form bonds with their teammates.

And by setting standards on after-hours communication, the members of your team can remain productive while still achieving work-life balance.

By helping the members of your team find their individual work-life balance you will strengthen your overall team culture. Show your team that finding balance is important by setting an example yourself. Make space for your team to have moments of fun throughout the day. And when using staggered hours, take advantage of the time you have together to encourage communication, while setting boundaries on long hours so that your team members can still achieve balance. By focusing a bit of your attention on helping your team members find their individual work-life balance, you will have a happier, healthier team.

CHAPTER 7

MENTAL WELL-BEING

As you work on creating a supportive culture for your team, you're bound to run into problems with the mental well-being of your team members from time to time. For a remote team, some of the situations you find yourself in will be similar to those in a traditional office. Others will be specific to your remote group. Either way, a remote team will need a remote-specific solution.

INTERPERSONAL PROBLEMS

Even with a tightly knit team and excellent communication, working remote can create feelings of isolation and anonymity. On occasion, these feelings can cause your people to handle problems or conflicts in a way they wouldn't normally. You may find yourself dealing with the challenge of unexpected interpersonal problems, such as apathy, trolling, or griefing.

Apathy

One of the most common interpersonal problems a remote team faces is simple apathy. One person has a question and drops it into the group chat, and a member of the team who knows the answer doesn't respond in a timely manner or, worse, doesn't take the time to respond at all. In a traditional office, simple apathy caused by a breakdown in communication is a lot more obvious. If one person verbally raised a question and didn't get a response, it would be clear that your team had communication problems.

For a remote team, apathy generally occurs because of communication breakdowns. Most of the time, tackling the problem of apathy with a remote group is as simple as proactively getting your people to talk and be engaged with each other. Create space and routines that encourage them to form bonds with each other.

Think about how the members of your group communicate best. For your remote team, averting apathy may be as easy as keeping your group chat lively or having a standing daily meeting for everyone to come face-to-face.

When the culture of your team is inclusive for all members, they will be less likely to be apathetic toward each other.

If cultivating healthy communication habits doesn't address the apathy problems you're facing, then what? Apathy has a number of different causes, depending on your team's work environment and dynamic. In order to counteract apathy, you need to know why it's happening. Remote apathy is most frequently caused by dysfunctional communication, but if that isn't the cause of the apathy you're seeing, you might be dealing with a situation that more closely mirrors one in a traditional office, such as apathy caused by losing interest in their work, or disliking their coworkers.

As you look for the cause of the apathy, be interactive with your group. Countering apathy isn't always going to be about building a good culture; sometimes it's going to be about being a good manager. Be there for your apathetic team member. Get to know him or her. Have frequent conversations. Find the reason for this person's individual apathy, and then find the solution that works specifically for that person.

Trolling

Worse than apathy is trolling. Trolling is when one member of the team says something that creates unnecessary frustration in a conversation or fans the flames of an already tense situation.

A while ago, a couple members of my team were having a debate in our group chat about where to get stock photos for a project they were working on. James had strong opinions about a service that he liked. But Olivia said she had already spent hours looking through that service, and it didn't have the right photos for her project. As James and Olivia discussed the project needs and their opinions, Carl chimed in to say that he didn't think our team should be responsible for sourcing stock photos to begin with. He pointed out that if the team wasn't required to source photos, James and Olivia wouldn't have to worry about what service to use to find them. But the team was responsible, and James and Olivia still needed to find a solution.

Carl wasn't adding anything helpful to the discussion. He was trolling. Olivia was frustrated about not being able to find what she needed, and James was working through the problem with her. Carl's comment didn't help them find a solution, but his misplaced venting did add to the frustration they were already feeling.

Trolling isn't always deliberate; trolling comments can be unintentional or just careless. It's easy to be engaged with a group chat and let your fingers type and hit enter before you've had a chance to really consider what you're saying. When a conversation is heated, with many people typing at once, you may find people responding faster than normal as they try to get their comment in before the conversation moves on.

Addressing trolling within your group is going to be a bit different than dealing with apathy. While a lot of avoiding apathy with a remote group is proactively encouraging bonds to form within your team, you will need to handle trolling on a case-by-case basis when you see problems arise. For the situation with Carl, I was able to pull him aside with a quick video call. Not only did this call his attention to his comment, but it gave him a moment to step away from the conversation with James and Olivia and cool down. Carl hadn't intended to troll the situation; his remarks stemmed from the frustration he felt when he would spend hours sourcing stock photos on projects with a short turnaround time. I listened to his concerns, and we were able to have a discussion and start working through his issue. With a little effort, I was able to help the team avoid short timelines for projects that required sourcing photos.

Griefing

A bigger problem than both apathy and trolling is *griefing*, a gaming term. When a gamer takes actions intended to give an opponent grief, that's griefing. Griefing in games can be overt, even aggressive. But for remote teams, griefing is much more passive-aggressive.

Natalie has three projects for three different account managers on a partner team that she needs to get done by the end of the day. Luke, one of those account managers, has been bugging her to handle his first because he wants to leave work early. The work that Natalie does on his project will impact how early he can finish his tasks. Luke asks for this type of preferential treatment often, and while Natalie could easily handle Luke's project first, she doesn't like the pressure he routinely puts on her. Natalie not only doesn't work on Luke's project first, but when she does wrap it up a few hours before the deadline, she holds off on sending it to him until the minute it's due. She knows that this will keep him at work late, but she does it anyway. This is griefing.

With a remote team, griefing can happen in a variety of ways: You may see a team member intentionally putting a coworker into a tough situation because of a previous conflict, or you might find someone withholding information because they're frustrated with the person asking the question. Griefing within a remote team can even be so passive as one person seeing a problem take shape, knowing that she could solve it, but allowing it to get out of hand because it isn't her direct responsibility.

Within your own team, creating strong bonds and mediating interpersonal conflict can mitigate griefing. But griefing with partner teams is a bit more common and tougher to address. One option would be to talk to the person about her behavior, but this may simply make her hide her actions rather than changing. When griefing happens with partner teams, the most effective approach I've found is to try to open up communication between the two groups. This could be setting up a video call where you mediate between the affected parties, Natalie and Luke, or inviting Luke and some of his coworkers to join your Storytime or Happy Hour.

Giving a face to the person on the receiving end of griefing can help relieve the problem. If video calls aren't common cross-team, your group may forget that the people on the other end of the project are working toward the same goal. Humanizing the conversations and bringing people together will help the bad behavior stop. When you are there, looking at each other, you gain a level of sympathy.

Griefing can be a tricky problem to spot. With Natalie and Luke, you might start looking for instances of griefing after Natalie complains about Luke repeatedly asking for preferential treatment. But griefing can be so subtly done with a remote team that it might be hard to know exactly when it's happening. Whether you directly see griefing in action or just suspect it, start working on strengthening your cross-team communication routines.

Interpersonal problems with a remote team can be challenging, but good communication can help you solve them. Be proactive in order to avoid apathy within your group, give immediate feedback to get to the root of trolling comments, and expand your communication routines to include partner team members when necessary to address cross-team griefing. By getting people to talk you will be able to solve a lot of remote-specific interpersonal problems.

STRESS

Take a moment to think back to a time when you felt a bit of work-related stress. It may have been because of the creative block you had on the project for that big account you were working on last month. Or it could have been yesterday before your budget meeting. How did you manage your stress?

Stress is part of everyone's life, but stress for people working remotely is amplified by isolation. In a traditional office, you can see when a member of your team is overwhelmed, and you can address the problem. In person, tension can be diffused. But sitting all alone in a home office, the silence can build and blow problems out of proportion. With your remote team, you may get lucky: The team member under stress may come to you asking for help. But what if she doesn't? How can you help her solve a problem you're unaware of?

Keep an eye out for stress building. Are you going into your busy quarter? Maybe workloads are approaching double what they are during your slow quarters. This will definitely add stress to your people. Are you seeing interpersonal issues more frequently? That is probably a symptom of a bigger problem that is adding stress to the members of your group. Are you noticing someone on your team consistently struggling to keep up with his or her workload? That's definitely going to add stress.

While tension can build when you're sitting alone, if you know how, you can also use the space of working remote to diffuse tension. After all, when you're alone in your kitchen, you have a great quiet place to take a few moments to breathe without being self-conscious. And for moments of minor stress, breathing can be exactly what you need to help yourself calm down.

When you're helping a member of your team work through a stressful situation, such as dealing with interpersonal problems or coming up against a small roadblock, encourage him to take a moment to breathe. A few deep, focused breaths can be enough to relieve the tension.

A few years back, Alex, a member of my remote team, reached out to me because he was feeling overwhelmed. The project he was working on was much larger in scope than the typical projects that my team undertook, and we'd just gotten off a call with the stakeholders where we expanded the scope even farther. The deadline was approaching, and Alex was worried that he'd reach the deadline unprepared. I knew the project well and knew that I could help him find a solution to finish on time, but he was so frantic about the expansion of the scope that I was having a tough time working with him. I needed him to calm down before we could solve the final challenges of the project together. What could I do? I knew that if he would take a few moments to breathe, he would be able to refocus his energy on completing the project.

When you offer advice on breathing, be genuine and speak from experience. If you don't already have breathing techniques that you like, put on your own oxygen mask first and do some research. If you're looking for a place to start, search "One Moment Meditation" on YouTube. It's a five-minute video that's a great introduction to basic breathing techniques. Stress can be overwhelming, and your team members may not be receptive to your help if they feel like focused breathing is an additional task to add to their to-do list or if it seems like you're being condescending with your advice. So, pass on your information, and if your breathing advice is something they want to look into further, they will.

For Alex, a few moments of deep breathing was exactly what he needed. I shared the link to "One Moment Meditation" and asked him to take a few minutes to breathe, maybe even to get some fresh air and call me back when he got back to his desk. Ten minutes later, we were able to come up with a strategy that helped him complete the project with a little time to spare.

For a team member who is dealing with stress caused by a creative block or even by a workload that has kept her at her desk for too many hours in a row, physically stepping away from the problem will help her come back to the project with fresh eyes. If you were in a traditional office, you could invite her to walk with you to the local coffee shop. But you're remote, so how can you help her to step away? Maybe recommend she go to the kitchen and brew a fresh pot of coffee, or invite her to take her dog for a 10-minute walk. Even simply stepping outside to see the sky and breathe fresh air can help relieve stress.

And if the stress is really just too overwhelming, and if you have the flexibility to do so, help your team member assess her responsibilities to see if there's the possibility of a flexible schedule for the day. Look at offering some staggered hours, or even a Sanity Day. (See Burnout, below.)

But wait, how do you spot someone who is dealing with this type of stress in the first place? Know what each member of your team is working on. If your group is working in an agile environment (see Chapter 3), you'll know the projects that are causing problems and be able to keep an eye out for when they become too much. The stress that comes from a creative block or a heavy workload can often create tunnel vision. The afflicted team member's comments in the group chat may be short tempered or seem out of character. Or the team member may even be notably absent.

With the great communication channels you've developed with the members of your team, you might even find that team members come to you when they're overwhelmed. Don't ignore the small comments you hear. They may be trying to not blow things out of proportion. But if it is important enough for them to mention, it's important.

Stress in the workplace is common. If you were managing a team in a traditional office, your tactics for helping your team work through stress would be different than the tactics you will need to help your remote team. Even though you're not in the same place, you still have tools to help your people. Whether it's simple breathing or giving them space to step away, by diffusing overwhelming tension you can help your team members stay level headed so they are in a position to solve their problems.

BURNOUT

Have you ever been working on a project where you just can't seem to see the light at the end? You keep putting in hour after hour and day after day, but around every corner the scope of the project seems to grow. You haven't had a good night's sleep in ages. And as you realize you're going into yet another sleepless night, you start to doubt your whole approach. Your brain is numb, and the stress is almost paralyzing. This is burnout.

Burnout happens when stress becomes so overwhelming that it causes physical and mental exhaustion. The impact of this exhaustion can cause insomnia, feelings of incompetence, forgetfulness, or a reduced attention span. Burnout can even be so physically depleting that it can cause increased vulnerability to illnesses like the common cold.

A common cause of burnout for remote workers is that the boundaries between work and life are easily blurred. When you work from home, not only are you always at home, you're always at the office. This makes it easy to have a sleepless night overthinking a project and fill the hours by working to put even more final touches on it. Not disconnecting from work for the night can cause a lot of extra stress and eventually lead to burnout.

Before burnout occurs for anyone in your group, keep your eyes open for things that may trigger it so that you can address it before it comes a problem. What are your team's pressure points? What situations routinely cause stress? Maybe you have individuals who chronically overwork by staying unnecessarily late or working weekends. Or you might have someone who is always allowing the scope of a project to grow into something overwhelming and unmanageable. When you are aware of the habits of your team members and the ways they are susceptible to stress, you'll be able to pinpoint how you can help each of them create habits that will reduce the chance of burnout. When you understand how they are ignoring their work-life balance, you will be able to help them acknowledge the need for it.

For the team member who chronically overworks, helping her avoid burnout may be as simple as defining your expectations on late-night or weekend work. Encouraging her to disconnect from work at the end of the day may help her recharge before she burns out. Or for that team member who's constantly under stress because the scope of his projects keeps growing into something unmanageable, you could coach him on how to define the objectives at the beginning of a project so he can maintain focus on the project goals without allowing the scope to creep.

Despite all of your efforts to help the members of your team find good work-life balance, there will be times when it just isn't something you can prioritize. You may have projects that need extra attention or have aggressive deadlines. Sometimes there is no way around stressful days that involve long hours. So what can you do then? Are all of your efforts to help your team find their individual work-life balance a waste of time?

Fear not! It's times like this when offering a sanity day may help. A sanity day is an extra day off to recuperate. Ideally it shouldn't use any paid time off. The member of your team has already put in a day's worth of hours: she or he just did it overnight or during the weekend. A sanity day is a day to completely disconnect from work. Encourage your employee to fight the urge to check in. And likewise, don't reach out to your employee for help on a sanity day.

Tyler, a developer on my team, was working on a large, high-profile project with an aggressive timeline and had put in long hours for the two weeks leading up to it. While his temper was getting short as the deadline approached, he was still dedicated to making the project a success. His work was still high-caliber, but it was clear he was looking forward to the weekend so he could recuperate from all the long days.

Tyler finished the project on a Friday afternoon in anticipation of a Monday launch date. But as Tyler was getting ready to log off for the weekend, the client sent through a last-minute direction change that would require him to overhaul a huge portion of the work he'd done over the previous two weeks. As soon as he heard the news of the new direction, he called me, completely overwhelmed. We talked through what the changes would entail, and while they were extensive, if he worked through the weekend, the project would still be able to launch on Monday as planned. But Tyler wasn't going to be able to take the weekend to recuperate, and I could see that he was facing burnout.

Rather than letting him become overwhelmed with missing his days off, I helped him schedule a sanity day, two in fact, for the Tuesday and Wednesday after the project launched. Knowing that he would have time to recharge changed his outlook of working through the weekend. His tone immediately brightened, and he was energized to tackle the new changes. He worked through the weekend and took Tuesday and Wednesday to recuperate. The sanity days helped him avoid burnout.

Sanity days can be rare but are especially helpful if you have someone who is putting in an unusual number of extra hours to reach a tough deadline. You might be able to arrange the day off with short notice—as soon as you see the initial signs of burnout. But if you're still in the thick of things, scheduling a sanity day for a future date just after your project wraps up will give your team member something to look forward to. Sometimes a sanity day is the best way to help individuals on your team maintain their overall work-life balance.

Whatever challenge your team members face with their mental well-being, there is a remote-specific solution to help you coach them. Be mindful of what your group is going through and search for creative solutions that suit your unique situation. Your approach to dealing with the emotional challenges your team faces defines how supportive your culture is.

CHAPTER 8

CAREER DEVELOPMENT

You've built a great culture. Your remote team is thriving, and the daily projects are going more smoothly than ever. Your group is happy! So, you're done, right? Well, not quite yet. We've been spending a lot of time talking about the aspects of culture that you can adjust with daily habits and communication, but a supportive culture isn't just focused on day-to-day routines. A supportive culture will also help your team members plan their career development and offer them opportunities to grow.

Career development is an ongoing process, and each member of your team will have a unique path they want to take. Helping the members of your team with career development can be challenging in any setting, traditional or remote. So, as a remote leader, how can you help your people learn more and be better at their job while planning for their professional growth? By focusing your efforts on mentoring them and recognizing their achievements as they grow, you will be giving them the support and encouragement they need.

With a remote team, both mentoring and recognition can be more challenging than they would be in a traditional office. But helping the members of your remote team with their individual career development isn't impossible. You've made it this far; I know you're up to the challenge!

MENTORING

Have you ever prepped for an annual review that didn't go at all the way you thought it would? I have. I had been working with Sarah, a member of my team, for a couple of years, and I thought I understood her career goals. I had no idea that with the extra hours she'd been putting in on special projects for the last year she had expected to get a promotion from junior to senior developer. If I'd have known, I would have been able to support and guide her in her efforts. But now, at this yearly meeting, I found that we weren't aligned at all. After we'd talked through everything, I left a bit disheartened because for the last year I'd thought we had a great dynamic going. And Sarah left frustrated, realizing that she had miscommunicated the intention behind her efforts, leaving her career growth unsupported for an entire year.

This scenario can happen in a traditional office; after all, miscommunications can happen anywhere. But for a remote team, miscommunications can happen more often. When face time is at a premium, getting all of the relevant information across can be difficult. Frequently, conversations can revolve around day-to-day projects and problems, with discussion of long-term goals being postponed until later. So, how can you build communication routines that will help you stay on the same page as your team members as they work on their career development?

One option is to proactively create a way to remain mutually transparent about the career goals of the people on your team. Working through an Individual Development Plan (IDP) with each of them can be an easy solution to understanding their goals and can give you a chance to lay out the expectations they need to meet in order to get to where they're wanting to go. Does your company already have a structure for creating IDPs? If so, that is a great thing to lean on. If not, don't worry. An IDP doesn't need to be complex; it can be as simple as hopping on a video call and together creating a shared document that lists long-term goals, the steps needed to get there, and any personal strengths the individual can lean on.

Let's look back at Sarah's situation. Moving from her current role as a junior developer to a more senior position would require her to to take more responsibility for communicating with the stakeholders of the projects she'd be leading. But her communication skills were weak. I needed to find a way to help her develop her voice.

By actively seeking out opportunities to mentor the individuals on your team, you can proactively help shape their skill set to match where they want to grow. Sarah, for example, didn't know that communication skills were such an important part of a senior developer position. But I did. So, I involved Sarah in projects, such as drafting a few stakeholder updates, that could present opportunities for her to learn, and in time she became better at communicating.

Mentoring, of course, isn't exclusive to remote teams. And many of the mentoring techniques used in a traditional office can translate to a remote team. But in a traditional office, finding opportunities to help your team members grow can be a bit less conscious; simply being in the same place can present opportunities for casual conversations about career growth and keep the goals of your team on your mind. As a remote leader, mentoring may take more of a conscious effort on your part.

Once you know what the individuals in your group are hoping to achieve, you'll be in a better position to help them. Understanding their goals can also give you an opportunity to guide them on a path you can support. I could have been in a situation where my team didn't currently need a senior developer. But I could still help Sarah with her communication skills. It would benefit her in the long run, and I would have a stronger employee. When a senior developer position did open up on my team, she'd be ready.

Once you and the individuals on your team have plans for their growth, build communication paths that will encourage them to come to you when they need advice. And likewise, build routines that will allow you to see when your team members are having a tough time with their goals. These paths may be very direct, such as weekly one-on-one meetings, which are a great time to talk about career goals and the challenges the individuals on your team are struggling with in trying to achieve them.

You may also find that some indirect communication paths can help you develop a good mentoring relationship with the people on your team. You are in a leadership role, and it's possible that the people who report directly to you may be intimidated by you. This isn't exclusively a remote problem, but working remote does take away some of the casual time together to get to know each other. A mentoring relationship involves trust between you and the individuals on your team. They can feel vulnerable when asking you for help or admitting they have a gap in knowledge.

Your participation in Storytime and Happy Hour (both discussed in Chapter 5) can help your team members become more comfortable talking candidly to you. They've seen your face; they know your demeanor. For example, if you've talked in Storytime about a recent situation that left you frustrated (maybe your roof leaked and you couldn't get roofers in to fix it before the big storm over the upcoming holiday weekend), your team would see how you handled a stressful situation. They'd learn that you can take problems in stride. Or if you've participated in a team-building game in Happy Hour, they may have seen how you can help them find creative solutions to problems while ultimately letting them own their decisions. Once your team gets to know who you are and how you react to situations, they are more likely to open up about their goals. They are more likely to come to you when they want to develop their skills. And you will be the one they turn to when they're struggling.

RECOGNITION

So, now you're really focusing on the career development of your team members. You're mentoring each one of them, and they have their individual paths planned out. They are each putting a lot of effort toward their success, and you're seeing a lot of actions that exceed their daily job descriptions. The members of your team are going out of their way to really shine.

Recognizing the members of your team for their successes will encourage them to continue doing great work. If the people in your group go out of their way to do something above and beyond, and their success goes unnoticed, they can become discouraged and might not try as hard to excel the next time they get the opportunity. But by supporting them and recognizing their success, you can help your team members stay focused and push toward their career development even when the steps they need to take get tough.

Nicholas, one of the developers on my team, found a bug in a snippet of code that was routinely used by my group. As part of each build process, my developers would manually go through and add a fix each time they used the snippet. But Nicholas found a few minutes to implement a solution that would remove the bug all together.

While Nicholas's work on this bit of code was relatively small, the impact it had on my team was great. The fix he implemented saved all of my developers a bit of time and removed the frustration they had every time they used that snippet of code.

Recognition is part of building a supportive remote culture. It will help your team feel seen and appreciated when it comes to difficult projects or big wins. It will show them that their accomplishments are significant to the larger group, that they are valued by the company. Working remote is isolating, but giving recognition shows your team their value and creates an inclusive environment.

In a traditional office you might already have structures for employee recognition, many of which may include in-person interactions or tangible rewards. Recognition might be a fancy lunch with the boss after a large initiative launches successfully or maybe a trophy that is passed from person to person, given to the one that completed the largest number of projects that week.

The same structures aren't generally in place for remote employees. The lack of recognition for a remote team can leave team members feeling forgotten, which can adversely affect morale. If someone has been putting in extra effort and it goes unnoticed, they may be less motivated to do it again. Calling out their successes can show them that you appreciate their extra effort.

How can you give recognition for your remote group? Could you send a gift card for a fancy lunch instead of needing to be in the same city to take them out? Is there a creative way you could digitally pass a trophy? Does your company already have traditional structures in place that you can adapt for your remote team?

Let's go back to Nicholas. What kind of recognition could I offer for his accomplishment? While the work he did to solve that bug in the code was not part of his daily responsibilities, the extra work and the impact that the change had on the team was still valued. But a gift card or trophy was disproportionate to the effort he put in. Giving grand recognition for such a small win would be insincere.

Recognition doesn't need to be tangible. Depending on the achievement, recognition could be as easy as giving your team member kudos in your next one-on-one or team meeting. For Nicholas, I shared with the group what he accomplished, discussed how it impacted the rest of the team, and thanked him for taking the time to go out of his way to make everyone's life a bit easier. It was a small act for me, but for Nicholas, it reminded him that I see his value as part of the team.

You can give recognition in a variety of ways, but you'll need to account for your team being remote. For Dave, who spent his weekend adding extra features to one of your newest products so that it would be ready to share with the client Monday morning, you could include a note in the next stakeholder update and give a brief showcase of the exceptional work that he did. Or for Emma, who has spent the last three months of nights and weekends in classes to learn a skill that your team was missing, you could send an email to upper management or include her accomplishment with your notes for Human Resources when you do her next Quarterly Review.

While recognition is often given for successes that are directly related to the job at hand, the members of your remote team will also have some personal wins that deserve attention. Recognition not only helps with career development by encouraging the members of your team to excel, it also directly helps you build your supportive culture. Recognizing the members of your team for the big events and wins that happen outside of work can show them that you value them. This recognition gives them a sense of belonging to the group because they are important not just for the hours they put in but because of who they are.

So, what are those big life events you could acknowledge? Maybe it's five years with the company or a promotion or change in title. Are there ways you can congratulate team members when they meet these marks? Maybe a team member just got married or had a baby. In a traditional office, it's easy to get your group to sign a card of congratulations. For a remote team it's a bit trickier to get everyone's signature on the same card, but it isn't impossible. We're all human, and giving recognition for things that deserve it will remind the members of your team that you see them as more than just hard workers. It will help them feel valued. It will help strengthen your culture.

Career development can take many forms, and with a remote team you will need to make an intentional effort. Finding the opportunities to mentor your team members and give them recognition for their successes will help you as you refine your team culture. Mentoring and recognition go hand in hand for going above and beyond to develop the growth, dedication, and sense of belonging for the individuals on your team. It's that one last step in building a fantastic culture.

CONCLUSION

Shaping your remote team's culture is up to you. It's time to shift to a remote-first frame of mind and adopt some remote-specific, culture-building processes. As you work on your team's remote culture, some of the new processes will feel natural while others may take more time to integrate into your routine. Be consistent. With a routine your team members can rely on, you will be able to create the supportive culture your team needs.

Implementing key culture-building processes will help you take control of your culture and shape it into the one you want it to be. Start with your team's communication routines:

- Approach your communication from a remote-first perspective and focus on processes that will allow your entire team to communicate together, no matter where they are working from. Create a culture that will support your team members and counter the feelings of isolation that can come from working remotely.
- Maintain transparency with your team members and relay the information they need in order to succeed. Being transparent remotely will take more of a conscious effort than it would if your team was in a traditional office. So, focus on transparency with your expectations, your team's processes and available resources, as well as what the success of each project looks like. Incorporating a project board and scrum, two elements of an agile workflow system, into your process can help you provide transparency to your team members about the projects they are working on.
- Get your team members in the habit of openly communicating with each other; good communication can build trust and enable collaboration. Communicate in real time; delayed communication can make your culture feel cold. And set a standard for quick face-to-face communication; not all video calls need to be formally scheduled.
- Develop routines that will encourage casual

conversations and frequent communication. Give your team members a space where they can laugh and joke together. Use communication routines such as Free Association Emoji, to get conversations started. Integrate community-building routines into your day with group activities like Storytime and Happy Hour; these activities will help your people feel like part of a team and will encourage friendships to form.

Building a supportive remote culture is an ongoing process. Once you find you have a happier and more productive team, celebrate a little! But, don't stop there. Keep looking at how you can further improve your team's culture.

- Remote workers notoriously overwork themselves, and boundaries for calling it a day aren't as clearly defined as they would be in a traditional office. Don't let the work day blend into the evening for your group. Help your team members find their individual work-life balance so they can continue to be happy and productive over the long term.
- From time to time, you may find yourself dealing with unexpected interpersonal problems among your team members, such as apathy, trolling, or griefing. Or you may have team members overwhelmed by stress or facing burnout. When mental well-being problems arise—whether they mirror situations that

you would see in a traditional office, or not—look for remote-specific solutions.

- A supportive remote culture will offer your team members opportunities to grow. Career development is an ongoing process, and each member of your team has chosen a unique path. Put in the time to help each member of your team with his or her individual career development.

Looking forward, remote teams are going to become even more standard. Technology is allowing us to be connected from farther and farther away. Today, remote teams may have members spread across different floors in the same building or different buildings on the same campus. Or remote teams may be like mine was: spread throughout different states across the country. The strategy of building a supportive remote culture and thinking remote first has such broad application; it could even be applied to space exploration. On a space station in orbit or during far-reaching expeditions, the relationship between astronauts and mission control is remote by nature. But it doesn't have to be isolating. With a remote-first approach, they can ensure a successful team culture. If we can all get into the habit of creating supportive cultures for our remote teams, we will be better prepared for whatever remote-work challenges the future holds.

If you run into some bumps in the road, that's okay. The personality of each team is unique and can evolve over time. If one of your favorite culture-building processes has stopped working, look for a way to shift it to suit your team's new needs. Get creative! And if you're really stumped, contact me for further guidance, I'm here to help. I want your remote culture to support every member of your team, including you.

You're ready to do this!

ACKNOWLEDGEMENTS

My first thank you is for Jared Watkins: You are my everything. Thank you for always listening and for using that brilliant mind of yours to remember everything I say. So many ideas would have been lost in the wind without you. Thank you for reading all of the words I put down on paper, even the bad ones (especially the bad ones). Thank you for being so encouraging. You made it possible for me to write this book; you make everything possible!

Patrick Pfeiffer, thank you for so selflessly sharing with me what you know about the world of self-publishing. You pointed me in the right direction and helped me find my groove (see what I did there :)

My brilliant editor, Pam Sourelis, thank you for helping me find my voice and making sure that I actually said what I was trying to say. You have taught me so much. I am a better writer because of you.

Those who read the manuscript—Jared Watkins, Mark Oblad, Nate King, Emily King, and Eddie Hodgson—thank you for your feedback and thoughtful comments.

My mentor for so many years, Tate Tozer, thank you for teaching me what being a great leader is all about.

My NDL team, I appreciate each and every one of you. Thank you for following me, trusting me, and making the workday fun. I have learned so much from all of you. Special thanks to you, Danh Hoang, for your insight; talking through the other side of the story brought me a fresh perspective.

The great Eddie Hodgson, thank you for always asking, encouraging, and believing. I like when I make you proud.

And Emily King, thank you for the chocolate. It has fueled me through the times when my thoughts wouldn't arrange themselves in an orderly fashion, consoled me when my words really just sucked, and reminded me that when times are tough great friends will always be there. Thank you for being a great friend.